WIZOO Quick Start

Mark Wherry

Cubase VST

(:wizoo:)

Imprint

Author   Mark Wherry
Publisher   Peter Gorges

Cover art   design box, Ravensburg, Germany
Editor   Reinhard Schmitz
Interior design and layout   Uwe Senkler

Order No.   WZ 00725
International Standard Book Number   0-8256-1915-7

Exclusive Distributors:
Music Sales Corporation
257 Park Avenue South, New York, NY 10010 USA

Music Sales Limited
8/9 Frith Street, London W1D 3JB England

Music Sales Pty. Limited
120 Rothschild Street, Rosebery, Sydney, NSW 2018, Australia

Printed in the United States of America
by Vicks Lithograph and Printing Corporation

Welcome

Like all Wizoo Quick Starts, this book is designed to help you get a handle on this topic as swiftly and easily as possible. To this end, the Quick Starts are written in concise, easy-to-understand language, and include CD-ROMs that provide you with hands-on experience.

This guide assumes that you have no previous Cubase knowledge and starts at the very beginning—which makes it ideal for two kinds of people. Firstly, new Cubase users daunted by the apparent size and complexity of the program, and secondly, those considering buying Cubase who want to know if this is the package for them—a fully working demo version is included on the CD-ROM.

Take the time to follow the tutorials as they've been written to show you Cubase from a practical perspective, rather than an arbitrary description of the features.

Here's hoping you enjoy reading, listening, and trying things out. Above all, I wish you lots of success learning the ropes!

Peter Gorges, Publisher

Table of Contents

Table of Contents

Setting Up Your Audio Hardware

1

The first step to be taken when you start using Cubase is to make sure everything is configured properly, enabling you to get the best possible performance from your equipment. This begins with the "Audio System Setup" dialog where all of the settings related to audio hardware are found. Whether you're setting up for first time or troubleshooting audio-related problems later on, the "Audio System Setup" dialog is the place to be.

❖ Select "Options > Audio Setup > System."

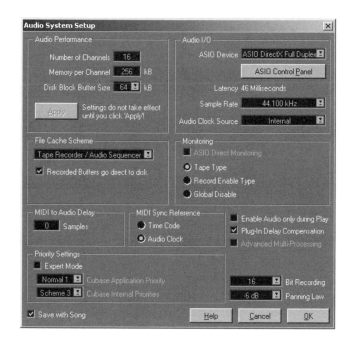

The "Audio System Setup" dialog.

PCI is an interface that allows expansion cards to "slot" into standard desktop computers.

A *USB* (Universal Serial Bus) connection on your computer allows you to plug a maximum of 127 devices on a single port. USB devices can be plugged in and out on the fly, meaning that you don't have to shut down your computer first.

FireWire is similar to USB, allowing up to 64 devices to be plugged in and out on the fly. However, FireWire is over 30 times faster than USB, which makes it ideal for audio and video applications.

ASIO (Audio Streaming Input Output) is a Steinberg innovation for getting audio into and out of the computer as efficiently as possible.

For the moment we're going to ignore most of the settings and leave them to their defaults. The most important first step is to tell Cubase what type of audio hardware we're going to use, whether it's the standard built-in hardware, an internally fitted extra *PCI* card, or a *USB/FireWire* device you've connected to the computer.

❖ Select your audio hardware from the pull-down *"ASIO Device"* menu in the "Audio I/O" group.

I Don't Have Any Extra Hardware

It's perfectly possible to use Cubase with only the standard headphone and microphone sockets on your computer, although you won't get any extra benefits such as low-latency and high quality converters.

What Is Latency?

Latency is the amount of time it takes to hear the result of an action you carry out; but what does this mean in practical terms? If you're using software instruments, where the sound is generated by the computer, the latency is the time it takes for you to hear the sound after pressing a key on your MIDI keyboard. Clearly the amount time from pressing a key to hearing the note should be so small it's unnoticeable, just like a standard MIDI keyboard with onboard sounds.

If you're recording audio into Cubase, a high latency will mean you hear what you're recording as much as a second after playing it! And if you're starting to think this is all a joke, welcome to the wonderful world of latency!

However, if you're relying on your computer's built-in features to make music, it's not all doom and gloom. If you're aware of the potential problems, it's easy to find ways to work around them.

An *ASIO driver* is a small piece of software that acts as a bridge between the audio hardware and the audio software. If you're buying new audio hardware, always check for the availability of ASIO drivers to ensure compatibility with Cubase.

The Monitoring Workaround

In an ideal world you would want to monitor the sound you're recording through the system it's being recorded with, but if the latency in your system is too high, this is not going to be possible. The solution is to monitor at the source instead of monitoring through the computer, and to disable monitoring in "Audio System Setup" before you start recording.

❖ Set Monitoring to "Global Disable."

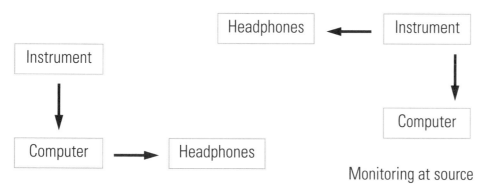

Monitoring through the computer

Monitoring at source

I Use a Mac

Because the Mac is an all-in-one combination of hardware and software, its standard built-in audio abilities are the best of any computer available. You should find that software instruments are playable, and monitoring through the computer may also be possible.

❖ The correct ASIO driver is usually chosen for you by default, "Apple Sound Manager."

I Use Windows

Since version 5, Cubase has shipped with improved DirectX ASIO drivers capable of supporting very low-latency if you're computer can cope with it.

Windows users are slightly less fortunate when it comes to the standard built-in audio hardware. It's not that the hardware itself is bad, but because Windows has to be able to cope with any type of soundcard you throw at it, performance trade-offs are inevitable. However, this situation is rapidly improving thanks to DirectX and other Windows technologies.

1 Select the "ASIO DirectX Full Duplex Driver."

2 If things don't appear to be working as they should, try the "ASIO Multimedia Driver" instead, which offers better reliability but with a higher latency.

What Else Do I Need to Know?

Cubase should now be ready to make some noise, but if you have any questions about the audio performance in Cubase, the following section is well worth reading.

How Many Audio Channels Do You Need?

Each audio channel within Cubase can play one track at a time, so if you want to record four separate instruments that playback simultaneously, you need to have four channels available, and so on.

The number of *audio channels* can be increased at any time by setting the "Number of Channels" parameter in the "Audio Performance" group. Cubase VST and Cubase VST Score can use a maximum of 72 audio channels, while Cubase VST/32 raises this number to 128, which should be more than enough for all the budding Peter Gabriels out there!

Audio channels are not the same as MIDI channels; they are purely for recording audio from the outside world. Having 16 MIDI channels available has nothing to do with the number of audio channels, and the reverse is also true.

The "Memory per Channel" setting lets you decide how much of your computer's memory (RAM) you want to allocate to every audio channel. Each audio channel requires a certain amount of memory to function, and the more memory you allocate to each channel, the fewer playback problems you will experience.

The "Disk Block *Buffer* Size" parameter lets you set the size of the buffer Cubase uses when accessing audio information stored on your hard disk. Again, the higher this value is, the smoother the ride. But be warned that a high "Disk Block Buffer Size" automatically requires a high "Memory per Channel" setting, so it can become something of a balancing act.

A *buffer* is an amount of memory used as an intermediate stage when data is moved around the computer. In Cubase, when files are played back, the data is read from the disk into the buffer and then read from the buffer into Cubase.

> Steinberg recommends setting the "Memory per Channel" to 256kb and the "Disk Block Buffer Size" to 64kb as a starting point.

When trying to get your head around these parameters, it's best to remember the saying, "If it's not broken, don't fix it." Sure it's a cliché, but the best advice is to go with the defaults and then allocate more memory if you start to run into problems. If you don't have the memory available, you'll have to use fewer audio channels.

The Sample Rate

For the mathematically inclined, the maximum frequency you can record is half the value of the sampling rate; so with a sampling rate of 44,100Hz (44.1kHz), the maximum frequency you can record is 22,050Hz. If this doesn't sound enough, bear in mind that we can only hear frequencies up to about 20,000Hz anyway.

The "Sample Rate" sets the range of frequencies you can record into Cubase and this figure relies totally on your audio hardware.

As with most numbers in the computer and digital audio worlds, the higher the sampling rate is, the better the end recording will be. However, the standard CD-quality setting of 44.1kHz is probably the one you will want to go with. Even if your card supports 48kHz I would still recommend using 44.1kHz because when you come to master your music for CD or MP3, you'll need to convert to 44.1kHz and quality can often suffer unless you're using the best of the best sampling converters.

Buffer Sizes on Your Audio Hardware

When we talked about latency earlier in this chapter, the conclusion was that to avoid latency you needed to get some extra, more specialized, audio hardware. Once this is plugged in and running with Cubase, you could still get latency, and if this is the case you need to lower the buffer size on the audio hardware's ASIO driver.

❖ Click the "ASIO Control Panel" button in the "Audio I/O" group. Mac users click the "Launch" button underneath the "ASIO Device Control Panel" label.

The dialog that appears is specific to the hardware you're using, so a trip to the manual of your audio hardware is in order. Look for references to buffer size and latency.

For PC users with no extra hardware, both the multi-media and DirectX ASIO drivers allow you to change the buffer size in the "ASIO Device Control Panel" to lower the latency.

Lower buffer sizes give lower latencies.

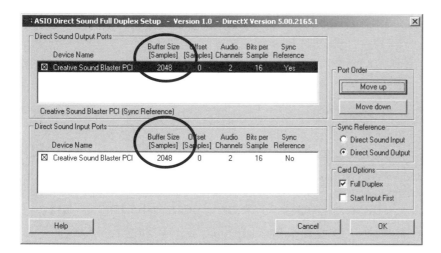

Lower buffer sizes put extra pressure on the processor, so start with the lowest buffer size your hardware supports and work backwards until there are no apparent audio glitches. Once again it's an issue of balancing and compromise.

First Steps with Cubase

2

The best way to get started with Cubase is having a song to experiment with. So with this in mind, we're going to load a song already containing some recorded parts.

1 Copy the "Demo Song" folder from the CD-ROM to a convenient location on your computer's hard disk.

2 In Cubase, choose "File > Open" and in the file selector, select the file "Demo Song/Demo Song 1" within the folder you just copied and click "Open."

The two key elements in Cubase are the Arrange window, where the song is constructed, and the transport bar, which provides controls for playing and recording the song. The Arrange window is split into four main parts: the track list, the arranging area, the Inspector and the toolbar.

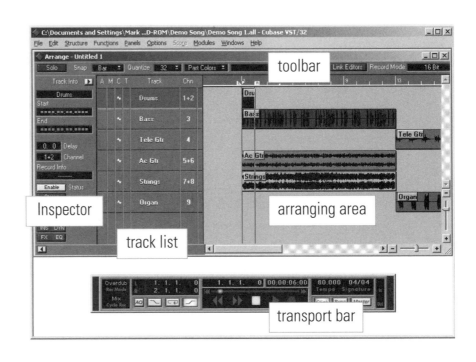

14

The track list, as the name suggests, is a list of the tracks that make up your song. Each track provides the space to record a line of music onto, and, generally speaking, you normally record each different instrument onto a separate track. Cubase supports different kinds of tracks for working with different types of musical information, but we'll be concentrating on the "audio" track type in this guide.

The arranging area is where your music is displayed as "parts," which are represented by rectangular blocks along a time ruler of bars and beats.

The Inspector

The Inspector lets you access parameters that are relevant to the currently selected track or part. For audio tracks and parts you can set the volume and pan, plus other controls for recording and mixing we'll look at later.

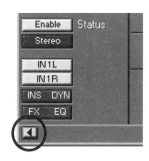

You can hide and show the Inspector panel by clicking on the Inspector icon.

When a track is selected, the parameters for that track are displayed in the Inspector—fairly simple. However, when a part is selected (regardless of which track is selected) the Inspector displays the parameters for that part instead. Because of this, it's possible to forget you have a part selected and think you are changing the settings for a track, when in actual fact you're changing the settings for a part. Try this:

1 With no parts selected, notice how the currently selected track is represented by the Inspector. At the top of the Inspector, the label "Track Info" will be displayed.

2 Now select any part on the arrangement and notice the Inspector's label change to "Part Info."

Numbering the Bars and Beats

The final piece of Cubase background I'll give you at this stage deals with the way Cubase numbers the bars and beats. This is useful to know because whenever you look at musical events in Cubase, their location in bars and beats is given as a set of four numbers that show bars, quarter notes, sixteenth notes, and ticks. For example, on the transport bar, the song position is given in just this way, as you can see in the picture below.

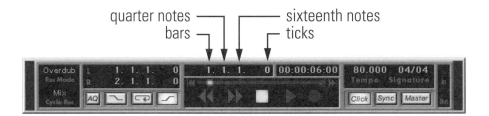

The bar number is fairly straight forward—it gives the number of the bar! Quarter notes reflect the number of quarter notes in the time signature, so for a bar of $^4/_4$ time, the sequence would be: 1.1.1.0 > 1.2.1.0 > 1.3.1.0 > 1.4.1.0 > 2.1.1.0. The sixteenth notes divide the quarter notes into four, so for a quarter note, the sequence would be: 1.1.1.0 > 1.1.2.0 > 1.1.3.0 > 1.1.4.0 > 1.2.1.0. Ticks divide the bar even further into thousands of tiny beats, but we won't need that level of precision at this stage!

If this all seems a little complicated, don't worry—it will become clearer as we work with the Arrange window in the next sections.

The Song Position Line

The demo song is a fairly simple 12 bar piece consisting of six tracks, and you can play the song by clicking the play button on the transport bar. As the song plays, the song position line moves across the Arrange window to illustrate the current playback position. When Cubase is stopped, the location of the song position line indicates where Cubase will start from when the play button is pressed again.

> The metronome click, useful as it sometimes is, can be disabled by deactivating the Click button on the transport bar, or by simply pressing Ⓒ on your computer.

To make the song position line jump to a new location, simply double click the new location on the time ruler if you're using Windows, or single click if you're on a Mac.

Locators and Cycling

In addition to the song position line, you'll notice there are two other markers on the time ruler which are known as the left and right locators. These have many uses in the program and one such use is to set the boundaries for cycle playback mode.

1 Set the left locator to bar 5 by clicking the left mouse button (or on the Mac, pressing ⎇ and clicking) along the time ruler at bar 5.

2 Set the right locator to bar 9 by clicking the right mouse button (or pressing ⌘ and clicking on the Mac) along the time ruler at bar 9.

3 Activate cycle mode by clicking the cycle button on the transport bar or by pressing ⌿ on the numeric keypad.

So long as the song position line is inside the left and right locators when you press play, Cubase will now play that 12-bar region indefinitely until the song is stopped or the song position line is moved outside of the locators.

> You can make the song position line jump to the left or right locator by pressing ① or ② on the numeric keypad respectively.

Using Shortcuts for Transport Controls

Once you've learned the shortcuts, you can hide and show the transport bar by pressing F12.

Learning the keyboard shortcuts for common transport controls can make you far more productive in Cubase. To play the song, press ⏎enter on the numeric keypad; to stop the song, press ⓪ on the numeric keypad. Pressing the ⓪ key a second time will move the song position line back to the left locator, if it's behind, or back to the beginning of the song, if it's in front. Pressing ⓪ when the song position line is at the left locator will move it back to the beginning of the song.

Moving Parts

Looking back at the Arrange window, two of the parts begin at bar 13 and it would be nice if we could move them back to the first bar so we can hear all the parts play together. To move a part, all you have to do is drag it with the mouse:

1 Drag the "Tele" part back so it begins at the first bar.

2 Drag the "Organ" part back so that it also begins at the first bar.

To drag multiple parts at a time:

1 Select multiple parts by shift-clicking them one at a time.

2 Now, when you drag a part, all of the selected parts will also be moved.

3 Try this now, making sure that you move the parts back to their starting positions when you're done.

Alternatively you can drag a box around them by clicking in an empty space and dragging a box from that position to highlight the parts you want to select.

Using the Snap Function

At this moment, notice how when you're dragging the parts around, they automatically move to whole bar positions—it's impossible to move a part so it starts on a half bar. In order to change this, we need to adjust the Arrange window's "Snap" value.

With "Snap" set to "Bar" on the Arrange window (the default value) you will only be able to move and perform other functions on parts at a whole bar resolution. It's possible to adjust the "Snap" value higher or lower, in

addition to turning it off completely, by clicking on the current "Snap" value and choosing a new one from the pop-up menu:

1 Click the current "Snap" value, which is currently "Bar."

2 Choose "1/2" from the pop-up menu.

3 The part can now be moved at half-bar steps.

Copying and Repeating Parts

When you play the song at the moment, you'll notice that the drums cut out after the first bar because the part only lasts for one bar. We need to make 11 copies of that part so the drums play over the full 12 bars.

❖ Holding down [alt]/[⌥], drag the part (as if you were moving it) to the second bar.

We now have drums that last over two bars, so we now need to make ten more copies. But in answer to the question you're now thinking—yes, there is a quicker way!

1 Select the drum part we just copied (the one in the second bar).

2 Choose "Structure > Repeat Parts," or press [ctrl]/[⌘] + [K].

3 Enter "10" as the "Number of copies."

4 Leave "Ghost copies" unselected.

5 Click "OK" or press [↵].

The drum loop is now copied to play over the full 12 bars.

When you copy parts containing audio, you're not making a copy of the audio file on the disk—the copied audio parts all play from the same file.

Merging Parts

With the row of one bar drum parts we've copied, it would be more convenient if we could join them together into one single 12-bar part.

1 From the toolbox, select the glue tool.

2 Click on the first drum part at bar one.

3 The part you clicked is merged with the next one.

You can choose different editing tools, such as the glue tool, in Cubase by accessing the toolbox.

On Windows, simply hold a right click in the arranging area, highlight a new tool and release the mouse button. On the Mac, use the Tools menu or press *ctrl* and click in the arranging area.

4 If you click the now two-bar part again, the same thing happens—the next part along is merged with the one you click on.

5 To merge all the parts on a track, hold down the *alt*/⌥ key and click the first drum part on the track.

6 When you're finished, select the arrow tool again from the toolbox.

21

Copying Multiple Parts

Let's now make three copies of the entire 12-bar 6-track section. We could select all the parts by shift-clicking or dragging a box, but a far quicker way is to press [ctrl]/[⌘] + [A] or choose "Edit > Select All."

With the technique described previously, use the "Repeat Parts" function to make three copies of this section by entering "3" as the "Number of copies."

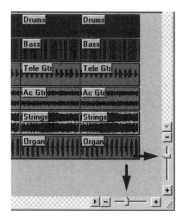

Getting It All to Fit on the Screen

Now that our arrangement has become bigger, you might not be able to see all 48 bars of it on the screen at once. To zoom in and out you can use the horizontal and vertical zoom controls located at the bottom right of the Arrange window.

❖ Adjust the controls until you can see all 48 bars along the horizontal.

Deleting Parts

To make our arrangement a bit more interesting, let's take out some of the parts so they're not playing all the way through.

❖ To delete a part, select it with the arrow tool and then press [⌫] (Backspace).

Now delete the first drum part and the first acoustic guitar part from the arrangement.

There is also a dedicated tool for deleting within Cubase, the eraser tool; clicking a part (or parts) with the eraser tool is another way to delete them. So, with the eraser tool selected, delete the the third string part and the third organ part from the arrangement.

> I prefer using the arrow tool for deleting as it's the tool I have selected most of the time. I find choosing the eraser and then returning to the arrow tool slightly more cumbersome, but thanks to the flexible design of Cubase, the choice, as they say, is yours!

Cutting Up Parts

Sometimes, you might only want to remove small chunks from a part instead of working with whole parts. Let's say we want to copy the last four bars of the string part to bar 33.

1 Copy a full 12-bar string part to bar 25.

2 Choose the scissors tool.

3 As you move the mouse around the arranging area, notice that a label on the toolbar shows the current position of the mouse along the time ruler.

4 Make a cut on the string part at bar 33 ensuring that the current mouse position is shown as 33.1.1.0 on the toolbar before you click to cut.

5 Delete the first part at bar 25, leaving us with the final four bars at bar 33.

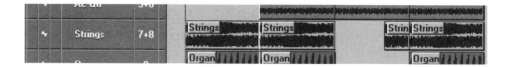

That was fairly simple, but often you'll want to make more complicated edits to the arrangement. For example, if we wanted to cut the acoustic guitar part at bar 25 into half-bar chunks, you might want to zoom in closer on that part.

1 Choose the zoom tool.

2 Click and drag a box over the region you want to zoom in on, which in this case is the acoustic guitar part lasting from bars 25 to 33.

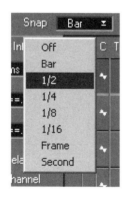

3 Now choose the scissors tool.

4 Cut the part into 24 half-bar sections. Remember, you'll need to set Snap to "1/2" on the toolbar to be able to cut at a half-bar resolution.

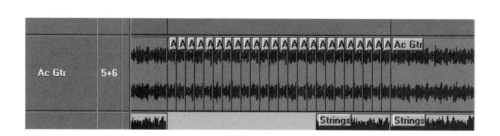

5 When you're done, select the zoom tool again.

6 Holding down the ⌈*ctrl*⌉/⌈⌥⌉ key, and click anywhere on the arrangement area.

7 The zoom level automatically reverts back to your original pre-zoom setting.

Muting Parts

We've looked at how to delete parts, but sometimes if you want to try out a new arrangement idea without permanently deleting any parts, it can be useful to mute the parts instead.

1 Choose the mute tool from the toolbox.

2 A part can be muted by clicking on it.

3 A part can be unmuted by clicking on it again.

4 Now, with the acoustic guitar part we cut into half bar parts, mute the second half of every bar. (You might want to zoom in on that part again to do this.)

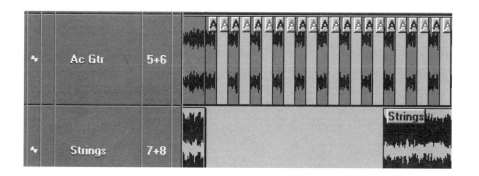

Notice how a muted part becomes grey in appearance and loses the waveform display.

If you like this new effect, something you may want to do is merge these half bar parts into one 12-bar part again, much as we did with the drum parts earlier.

1 We'll use the glue tool to do this, but when a muted part is merged in this way it becomes active again and the effect is lost.

2 To combat this problem, first delete the muted parts.

3 Select the glue tool.

4 Clicking on the acoustic guitar part at bar 25, merge it with the other parts and stop when your screen looks like the picture on the left.

If you want to practice further, try copying an organ part to bar 25 and then chop it up as we did the acoustic part and mute, delete, and merge as you like.

> If you want to mute an entire track, you don't have to use the mute tool and click on every single part. Instead, simply click in the "M(ute)" column of the track you want to silence on the track list. A large dot appears to illustrate this track is muted.

Soloing Tracks

The solo function on the Arrange window is useful when you want to hear one track in isolation from the rest of the arrangement:

1 Select the desired track in the track list.

2 Click the big red "Solo" button on the toolbar.

> Notice how all the other tracks become automatically muted when the solo button is active.

Introducing the Channel Mixer

3

The Channel Mixer loosely resembles a traditional mixing console with faders to control the level of each track, pan pots to control the stereo position of a track, mute and solo buttons. Note that the mute and solo buttons on the Channel Mixer have no effect on the mute and solo buttons found on the Arrange window—they are completely independent.

❖ Open the "VST Channel Mixer" by selecting "Panels > VST Channel Mixer 1" or by pressing `ctrl`/`⌘` and `*` on the numeric keypad.

The mixer channels run consecutively from left to right, and this is important to remember. The order of the channels on the mixer does not follow the order of the channels on the Arrange window; it's only a matter of convenience that they both start off this way.

Because our song ("Demo Song/Demo Song 1") contains both mono and stereo tracks, the mixer displays both mono and stereo channels.

If you look at the Panels menu, you'll notice Cubase offers two VST Channel Mixer windows. This is because each mixer window can be configured to show different sets of faders by clicking on the "View" tab in the control strip at the left of each window.

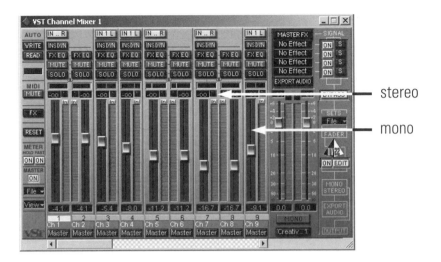

stereo

mono

❖ The left and right faders on stereo channels are linked by default—try moving the left or right of a pair and you'll see what I mean.

❖ To move either the left or right channel independently, drag the fader with the [alt] key held down. Note that as soon as you drag a left or right fader without [alt], they become linked again.

❖ The pan settings are independent for the left and right channels, and are panned hard left and hard right respectively by default.

To the far right of the "VST Channel Mixer" is the Master section, which represents the final stereo signal that comes out of the computer to your speakers. Although this section can be displayed in its own window ("Panels > VST Master Mixer" or [ctrl]/[⌘] and [+] on the numeric keypad), I like to have it displayed in the "VST Channel Mixer" by activating the "Master On" button in the control strip on the far left.

I've already set-up a basic mix with levels and pans, but feel free to adjust these settings and come up with your own mix by simply moving the faders and pan controls to get a feel for the process.

To reset the volume fader to 0*dB*, or the pan control to center, ⌜ctrl⌝/⌜⌘⌝-click the relevant fader or control.

At its most basic, the point of mixing is to achieve a good balance of all the tracks, making sure that nothing distorts and overloads, and while the level meters and overload indicators are useful, they are no substitute for your ears.

Although it's true that digital mixing systems are less forgiving than their analog counterparts, you can push them surprisingly far. If you're getting red lights, always solo those channels to check the sound isn't distorting, and then pull the faders down if necessary. The trick is to keep the master fader at 0dB while moving the individual channel faders so the master levels don't overload.

> Unfortunately the VST Channel Mixer can't use the names from the Arrange window, so you'll need to rename the channels by clicking the default "Ch x" labels, typing a new name, and pressing return.

The level of sound is measured in decibels (*dB*). While 0dB implies that there is no sound at all, on a mixer it means that when the signal comes through a fader, there will be no increase or decrease of the level, which is why it's the default position.

Making Your First Audio Recording

4

Recording audio into Cubase, whether it's a guitar, vocals, or something similar, is fairly simple; though a small pre-record ritual must be undertaken the first time you record a track on a new song.

To create a new song, choose "File > New" or press [ctrl]/[⌘] + [N].

Setting Up the Arrange Window

You can rename a track by double clicking on the name in the track list, typing a new name, and pressing [↵].

Although more than one track can be assigned to the same channel, a channel can only playback one piece of audio at a time. Each different instrument you record should be put on a different channel.

1 On the Arrange window, select the track you want to record onto.

2 If there are no more free tracks available, a new track can be created by selecting "Structure > Create Track" or by pressing [ctrl]/[⌘] + [T].

3 If the track isn't already set to the audio track type, do this by clicking in the "C(lass)" column and choosing "Audio Track" from the menu.

4 Set the track to the required audio channel by clicking in the "Chn" column and choosing the channel from the menu. Example: An audio track set to channel one will play and record through channel one on the "VST Channel Mixer."

Setting Up the Inputs

❖ Open the "VST Inputs" window by selecting "Panels > VST Inputs."

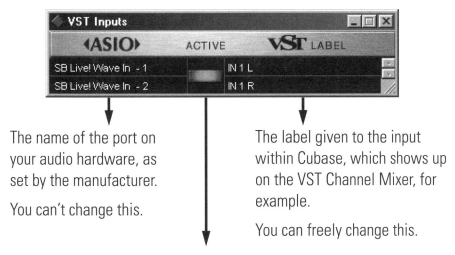

The name of the port on your audio hardware, as set by the manufacturer.

You can't change this.

If this button glows bright green, that pair of stereo inputs is active.

The label given to the input within Cubase, which shows up on the VST Channel Mixer, for example.

You can freely change this.

This window shows a list of all the audio inputs available to Cubase. If you're using your computer's built-in audio hardware, there will only be a single pair of inputs. But if you have a card with multiple inputs, the display will show all the pairs of inputs that are available.

If you don't see all the inputs you're expecting, check the user guide that came with your audio hardware because the ASIO driver often has its own control panel allowing pre-Cubase configuration of the hardware; this is especially true of hardware from companies such as MOTU and RME.

> To get to an ASIO driver's control panel, open the Audio System Setup dialog ("Options > Audio Setup > System") and click "ASIO Control Panel."

❖ Activate the inputs you will be using by clicking the green buttons to enable and disable each pair of physical inputs as required.

If you have a system with multiple inputs, only activate the input pairs you are actually going to use as each active input requires a small amount of valuable processing power.

Renaming the Input Labels

By default, the names assigned to the inputs aren't very meaningful. So it's a good idea to give them more sensible labels, especially if you have multiple inputs and they stay connected to the same devices such as microphones, mixers, keyboards, or guitars.

1 Rename an input by clicking the label.

2 Type in a new name.

3 Press ↵.

With the inputs set-up, close the "VST Inputs Window" and we're ready to assign them to audio channels on the "VST Channel Mixer."

Assigning the Inputs

Assigning audio inputs to audio channels is the process of saying to Cubase, "I want my microphone, which is plugged into this input on my audio hardware, to come through on this audio channel of the mixer for recording and playback."

1 Open the "VST Channel Mixer" ("Panels > VST Channel Mixer 1" or [ctrl]/[⌘] and [∗] on the numeric keypad).

2 At the top of each channel strip is an input button.

3 Clicking the darker region to the right of the input button displays a menu so you can choose the audio input to use for that channel.

4 Alternatively you can click in the lighter region of the input with ctrl/⌘.

Notice how the audio input's menu shows all the inputs we activated in the "VST Inputs" window, along with any labels we changed.

> You can also find an input button, which functions just the same as the one described above, on an audio track's "Inspector Panel" within the Arrange window. Sometimes, if you just want to assign a single channel, it maybe more convenient to use this one, rather than open up the "VST Channel Mixer."

Setting the Right Level

Monitoring is when you listen to an audio signal being played live, usually before or during the recording process. We discussed this subject in more detail back during the first chapter on page 9.

The input button can, as we've just seen, be used for assigning inputs. But it has a double function as you can also use the same input button to enable and disable monitoring on a given audio channel.

1 Enable monitoring on a channel by clicking the left side of the input button on either the "VST Channel Mixer" or the Arrange window's "Inspector Panel."

2 The input button lights up when monitoring is activated.

When monitoring is activated, a second "In" button also lights up on the channel strip.

The level meters on the "VST Channel Mixer" usually show the audio output level. But when this second "In" button is illuminated the level meters show the audio input level instead. It's important to remember this as the "In" button can be enabled and disabled independently of the input button by simply clicking on it.

When you're monitoring the signal, make sure that the "In" button is lit. Although the "In" button should later be disabled automatically along with the input button, if on playback when you hear a channel playing but see no activity on the level meter, the "In" button has probably been left on by mistake.

Before you record anything, you always need to monitor what you're intending to record for the purpose of setting a good level and to check that the signal isn't going to clip. Even if you're unable to monitor the audio through Cubase, you should still activate the "In" button on the level meter to check that the incoming signal doesn't go into the red.

You could write an entire book on the subject of recording alone, but the general idea is to get the level as hot (which is recording speak for loud!) as possible without distortion. Even if you're recording something that will ultimately be fairly quiet in the final mix, you still want to record it as loudly as possible. This is actually one of the most common mistakes people make when they start out, recording with only about 20% of the level meter lighting up—it should be at least 90%!

Another important point to remember is that moving the faders on the "VST Channel Mixer" alters the output level and not the input level, meaning that the faders have no effect on your recording level whatsoever. To increase or decrease the level of the input signal you're recording, you need to adjust the volume at the source, for example, the output volume of your keyboard, guitar amp, or microphone pre-amp.

Setting Up the Tempo, Metronome, and Count-in

It's important to play to a metronome click when you're recording because it will be difficult, if not impossible, to do further editing at a later stage if you don't. To set the desired tempo of your song:

If you don't hear the metronome click, make sure the Click button is active on the transport bar. If it isn't, click it or press Ⓒ to turn the metronome click on.

1 Double click the "Tempo" value on the transport bar, type in a new value, and press ⏎.

2 Play the song with the metronome click active to check whether that will be a good tempo or not.

A count-in is the number of bars Cubase gives you from the point you hit the record button to when the recording actually starts. By default this is two bars and you'll only hear the metronome click during this period. If you want to change these settings:

1 Double click the "Click" button on the transport bar to open the metronome dialog.

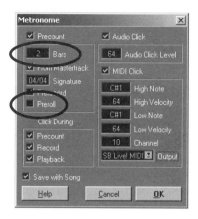

2 The "Bars" parameter in the top left sets the length of the count-in.

3 If you want to hear the preceding music during the count-in, activate the "Preroll" flag.

You'll notice this dialog also allows you to configure the metronome click by letting you toggle both the Audio and MIDI click. The Audio click is useful if you're not using a MIDI sound source. If you have a soundcard with onboard sounds or a keyboard or sound module hooked up to your computer, you can use the MIDI click instead of the rather shrill-sounding alternative. Click "OK" to close the dialog when you're happy.

Recording the First Track

With the input assigned to the right channel, the recording level set, and the tempo, count-in and metronome perfected, we're ready to record our first track.

1 Click the "Enable" button on the Inspector Panel to enable this track for recording.

2 The first time you enable a track for recording on a new song, a file selector will appear for you to choose the path for the recordings to be saved to.

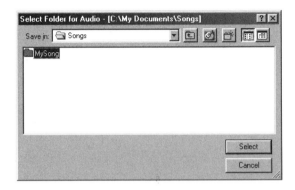

3 It's a good idea to save each song in its own folder and keep all the song and audio files in this folder.

4 Set the left locator to the point you want to start recording, and the right locator to the point you want to end the recording.

When "punch out" is active, the recording process will automatically stop when the right locator is reached.

5 If you don't want to set a definite end point for the recording, make sure the right locator is set further along than the left and disable the "punch out" button on the transport bar (see picture below).

6 When you're ready, simply click the record button on the transport bar, or press [*] on the numeric keypad.

7 When you've finished recording press the stop button, and that's all there is to it!

Recording in Stereo

If you want to record a stereo input on one track, such as the output from a keyboard:

1 Select the track you want to record in stereo.

2 Click the "Mono" button on the "Inspector Panel" so that it changes to "Stereo." (Note that on the Mac, this button is always labeled as Stereo, but is inactive if the track is set to mono.)

However, you can only activate a stereo track if:

1 The channel the track is set to is an odd number (even channels are automatically locked as mono channels).

2 The track is empty (tracks that already contain audio parts are also locked as mono channels).

3 The next channel is not set to a track containing audio parts. For example, even if a track set to channel 3 contains no audio parts, but another track set to channel 4 does have some audio parts, both tracks will be locked as mono channels.

Stereo tracks work by linking two channels together, as you can see on the "VST Channel Mixer." So you effectively loose a channel when you activate a stereo track.

Adding Effects to Your Recording

5

One of the most amazing features of Cubase is described by the three additional titles in the product's name, VST. VST is an acronym for Virtual Studio Technology, a feature-set that allows you to run an entire studio from inside your computer with no extra hardware. In the last chapter we've already been using one feature of VST, the ability to act as a multi-track recorder. But VST goes much further than this by providing a mixing desk, effects, equalizers (EQs), virtual instruments, and more.

This chapter shows you how to use some of the virtual effect features within Cubase. We're going to use the arrangement we made in a previous chapter, but you can cheat if you like and load "Demo Song/Demo Song 2" from the CD-ROM.

About Insert and Send Effects

A *wet* signal refers to one that contains some processing by an effect, a *dry* signal is one that doesn't.

There are two ways an effect can be used—as a "send" effect, or as an "insert." When an effect is used as a "send," a proportion of the signal is sent to the effect and the *wet* output from the effect gets mixed with the original *dry* signal. When an effect is used as an "insert" effect, the whole signal goes through the effect so only the *wet* signal is used.

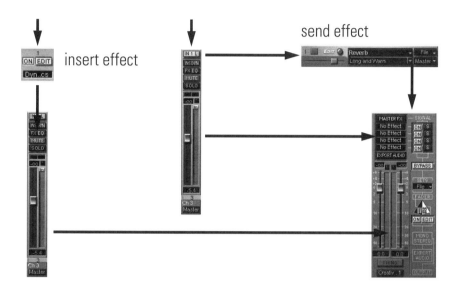

An important point when it comes to resources is that send effects can be used globally by all tracks, whereas insert effects only apply to one particular track.

Although there are no strict rules about which types of effects should be run as sends or inserts, there are some general guidelines. Most importantly, sound transformation plug-ins such as dynamics (compressors, limiters, expanders and gates), EQs and filters, should be run as inserts. Reverb is almost always used as a send effect and delay and modulation effects can really run on either, depending on the situation.

Using Send Effects

We're going to add some reverb to our mix. To do this we'll set up a reverb plug-in as a send effect.

1 Open the VST Effects window, a virtual effects rack within Cubase, with "Panels > VST Effects."

2 Click the "No Effect" label and select "Reverb" from the pop-up menu listing all of the plug-ins installed on your system.

click to open the effect's editor

power button
(on by default)

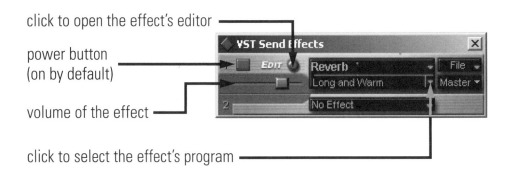

volume of the effect

click to select the effect's program

With the effect ready to go in our virtual effects rack, we now need to send signals from the Channel Mixer to that effect.

1 Open the Channel Mixer.

2 Choose the channel you want to add the effect to and click that channel's "FX/EQ" button.

3 You'll notice that the "FX/EQ" button is duplicated in the inspector panel when an audio track is selected on the Arrange window.

4 The Channel Settings window opens and displays settings relevant to a particular channel on the Channel Mixer. Although many elements of the Channel Mixer are duplicated, this window provides access to the inserts and sends, as well as the built-in EQ and dynamics you might like to explore on your own.

5 To send a signal from this channel to the effect we have set up, we're going to use the send controls.

6 Cubase automatically patches the send controls to the effects set up in the rack, so the first send control is patched to the Reverb plug-in we just set-up.

7 Enable the send control by activating the "ON" button.

8 Use the rotary control to set the amount of signal that is going to be sent to the Reverb unit. The higher the value is, the more of that effect will be mixed to the original sound.

The most important thing now is to play the song and experiment with adding the Reverb effect to other channels in this way and to listen to the overall sound as you change the parameters, especially the amount of each signal being sent to the Reverb plug-in.

What does the "PRE" button do? PRE is an abbreviation for "pre-fader," and when this button is activated the signal is sent to the effect before it reaches the fader. Normally the signal is sent post (or after) the fader, which means that the amount of signal sent to the effect is proportional to the volume of that channel.

When you're happy with the general idea, following the same procedure, try adding the Chorus plug-in as a send effect and start by applying some chorus to the acoustic guitar channel.

Clicking the longer blue "FX" button in either the Channel Mixer or Channel Settings windows is a handy way to bring up the VST Effects rack.

If you want to do a quick comparison with and without send effects on a particular channel, rather than having to deactivate each send individually simply enable the BYPASS button. Although the ON buttons remain active, the actual sound is bypassed until the BYPASS button is disabled.

Using Insert Effects

If you had a good look around the Channel Settings window, you'll have noticed that this also includes the controls for setting up insert effects on a particular channel. Let's add the Overdrive plug-in to the electric guitar.

1 Locate the "Inserts" on the Channel Settings window for the Tele Gtr.

2 Click the "No Effect" ("No E..ct") label and choose "Overdrive" from the pop-up menu of effects.

3 With insert effects you have to remember to switch them on, so click the "ON" button to activate the effect. Toggling the "ON" button allows you hear the guitar track with and without the effect.

4 Click the "EDIT" button to open the editor for the insert effect, in this case Overdrive.

5 Edit the parameters or choose a preset from the preset pop-up menu by clicking on the little arrow button.

Troubleshooting

6

Running Out of Gas

Effects plug-ins are one of the biggest performance drains on your processor when working with Cubase, and there will come a moment when the system simply runs out of gas and you run into problems. To monitor system performance you can open the VST Performance indicator ("Panels > VST Performance").

The "CPU" row indicates the load on the processor and if the red light starts to flash, you're trying to do more than your computer can handle. It can be useful to keep this indicator on the screen, especially when working on complicated mixes.

The "Disk" row indicates the performance of your disk drive. The more tracks you read from the disk at the same time, the more pressure you put on your storage device. If you're running out of gas on the disk side of things, try defragmenting (consult your computer's manual about this) and, if that doesn't help, reduce the number of tracks or buy a faster drive.

FAQ

7

I've finished my mix and I want to create a CD or upload my song to the Internet. What can Cubase do to help me?

Cubase provides a feature called "Export Audio" that automatically creates a file containing everything you would normally hear through your speakers when you play the song in Cubase. This file can then be used by your regular CD writing software (such as Toast, EZ CD Creator, Nero, and so on) or an MP3 encoder to create an MP3 file that can be uploaded to the Internet.

1 Set the left locator to the start of your song and the right locator a couple of bars after the end of your song. This is to allow for the "tail" sound of effects such as reverb or delay.

2 Choose "File > Export > Audio Tracks" and type a name for the file.

3 Set the file type to "Wave" on the PC and "AIFF" on the Mac.

4 Set Resolution to 16-bit, Sample Rate to 44.1kHz, and Channels to "Stereo Interleaved."

5 Make sure all three "Include" flags are checked: "Automation," "Effects", and "Master Effects."

6 Click "Create File" and wait for the magic to happen!

CD-ROM Contents 8

On the CD-ROM that accompanies this book you'll find a collection of essential resources for both Mac and Windows platforms, including:

The »Demo Song« Folder

This folder contains materials used in the tutorials and should be copied to your computer's hard drive.

A Demo Version of Cubase VST/32 v5

If you don't yet own a copy of Cubase and are using this guide to get more familiar with the package, this save-disabled (but otherwise fully functional) demo will let you work through the tutorials without having to make any extra purchase.

A Collection of Freeware VST Effects Plug-ins

The plug-ins bundled with Cubase provide plenty of sonic possibility, but we've included some of the best free plug-ins around for those who just can't get enough! Follow the instructions included on the CD-ROM for details on how to install the plug-ins if you get stuck.

Internet Links

The official site for Cubase (http://www.cubase.net/) includes video interviews with high-profile users like Phil Collins, and a forum to discuss your problems, the ones relating to Cubase of course, with the rest of the world. Steinberg's full web presence (http://www.steinberg.net/) provides product information, a knowledge base, upgrades, and more.

If you're a Mac Cubase user, join the Mac VST mailing list (http://groups.yahoo.com/group/vst-mac) today for helpful and friendly advice. Be sure to also visit the Hangar (http://www3.sympatico.ca/the-kid) for news, articles, OMS patchnames, and more.

A mailing list for both Mac and PC platforms is at http://groups.yahoo.com/group/cubase and they also have a great resource page (http://www.cubasefaq.com/). The Cubase web ring (http://www.dbrown.force9.co.uk/webring.html) is another great place for Cubase resources.

You can read the latest music technology news and find some Cubase tutorials at http://www.studioinabox.co.uk/ And then there's http://www.mp3.com/markwherry ... well, what can I say?